REALITY CHECK
POETRY OF LIFE
ANTONI CHUCK

FAILURE SUCCESS

T0019590

Reality Check

Reality Check

Poetry of Life

Antoni Chuck

iUniverse, Inc.
Bloomington

Reality Check
Poetry of Life

iUniverse books may be ordered through booksellers or by contacting:

iUniverse
1663 Liberty Drive
Bloomington, IN 47403
www.iuniverse.com
1-800-Authors (1-800-288-4677)

ISBN: 978-1-4620-2940-2 (pbk)
ISBN: 978-1-4620-2941-9 (ebk)

Printed in the United States of America

iUniverse rev. date: 06/27/2011

Contents

Contents

Part Two: Poverty & Greed

Contents

Part Three: Revolution

Part Four: Reality Check

Letter from the Author

First off, I would like to thank God for blessing me with the gift of writing. I would also like to thank all who made the publishing of my first collection of poetry possible, either through reviewing, inspiring, helping with my development as a writer, or directly or indirectly providing support and opportunities. Thank you to Lloyd Chuck, iUniverse, Keshia Mamdeen, the Haniff family, Mr. Duffin, Mrs. Mackenzie, Mr. T. Jones, Mr. Watts, Miss Inniss, Mr. Gaskin, Grandma, Grandpa, Monahki Entertainment, and the rest of my family and friends. Last but not least, I would like to thank you, the reader, for giving me a chance by purchasing my first book. I really and truly appreciate it, and I hope this is the first of many. Thank you, and I hope you enjoy the book as much as I enjoyed writing it.

PART ONE

Love and Loss

Key

Endless Tale

Living

Suspicion

More Than Ever

Break Up

Loneliness

Lonely Old Lady

Always Remember

Back to Me

Butterfly

Accept or Decline

Special Treatment

Real One

Accidental Love

A Song by the Heart

Best Foot Forward

Beauty Comes Naturally

One Stop Short

The Girl I Never Met

A Little Miracle

First Cry

Grandma

Believe in Music

Dear Nicole

First Time

Crazy Chick

Love Light

Birthday Sex

Beyond Friendship

Introduction

Things I Would Do for You

Doubts

Words of the Wise

Simplicity

Perfection Is You and I

Thick and Thin

3:04 a.m.

Sooner Than Later

Gone

Happily Ever After

Key

Pieces of my heart remain in the past.
A piece was left with each of my family members,
Each of my childhood crushes.

My happiness appears to be hidden away in certain songs.
Many artists hold the key.

Memories of a happy time,
Memories so innocent.
Lost faith in who I can be.
Need inspiration,
And someone from my past is the key.

Endless Tale

As the piano plays,
The keys inspire emotions,
Bringing up thoughts:
Feelings of you and I.

A long, depressing theme,
A short description of the agony my heart feels.
Words reflect my feelings.
Teardrops fall as my soul bleeds.

An empty space
Yet to be filled:
The endless tale of love and heartbreak.

Living

I'm looking at them,
Thinking, "That's how we used to be."
She caught me staring
But pretended like she didn't recognize me.
Judging by his body language, he figured out who I was.

No words,
Just glares.
It kind of hurt how she ignored me.
Oh well, this is my stop.
I guess we will continue living.

Suspicion

Her actions are suspect.
Her reasons don't make sense.
What could've changed in such short time?
What would make her want to leave?

In the blink of an eye, things just changed.
Don't know what happened,
No explanation,
She just woke up and decided she had had enough.

She spoke her mind in a text,
A text I didn't pay any attention to because I was busy.
Got home that night to find she was really gone; she took
everything.

Something is wrong with this picture.
I can feel it in my stomach.
We didn't fight.
I don't remember doing anything wrong.
I can't figure out why she would leave.

We were supposed to get married,
Start a family.
We had our whole life planned.
What could have changed?

Reality Check

Found a note in the bed,
A note I wish I never read.
It said she found someone else,
Someone who loves her more than I did.

Words as cold as a winter day,
Details as sharp as a butcher's knife.
How could she do this to me?
Didn't even have the courage to leave with a decent
goodbye.

The scent of the ink,
The color of the paper:
You can tell she meant to hurt me.
She wanted me to suffer.

She was my world.
I thought I was her all.
She's been cheating on me since day one.

She didn't value what we had.
She left me in pieces.
My heart tells me to go grab my piece,
To find her and every guy I suspect she has been with and
Do what O. J. did.
But then I come back to reality.

More Than Ever

Been shot in the leg,
Stabbed in the back,
Yet I've felt no pain greater than when you left me alone
that night.

Been thinking,
Been trying to come up with excuses for you,
Trying to convince myself,
Make me believe something is wrong with me.

Been screamed at,
Been ignored,
But for some reason, it hurts more now than ever.

Break Up

Sporadic emotions:
I can't control my feelings.
I'm helpless when it comes to you.

I tried changing my ways,
Tried doing what's best for us,
And realized what's best for us is only working for you,
'Cause I don't feel like I'm being myself.

Believe me, I love you.
But we're not working out.
I want the best for you,
And you can only get that if we go our separate ways.
It would be best if we broke up and forgot each other's
names.

Loneliness

Have you ever just sat and wondered,
Thinking "What if?"
Wishing that you had someone to share life with?

Going home to a lonely house,
Unhappy, without a home.
No one to share love and laughter:
Just silence and loneliness.

Have you ever awakened in the middle of the night,
reaching out to someone,
To find you have nothing but pillows by your side?

Have you ever had the urge to try new things, go new
places,
But you have no one to share such adventures with?

I want to be your other half.
Let me take care of you.
Let me be the reason that loneliness forgets who you are.

Lonely Old Lady

I look into her eyes, and I see sorrow.
I wonder what it is like to be her age,
Knowing I might not wake up tomorrow.

No grandkids,
No loved ones.
All I got is my daytime strolls,
A nurse who thinks very little of me,
And pills that tell me when my eyes should be closed.

I don't know if I could live like that,
Don't know what I would do.
All I know is that I respect that lonely old lady
For getting out of bed every morning.

Always Remember

On a cold winter day,
On a cold winter night,
Nothing but snow in sight:
Only thing I'm missing is you by my side.

Reminiscing of nights when we used to shack up,
Watch movies,
And make love.

Now those days are gone,
And I'm left in the cold.
Hot chocolate doesn't taste the same anymore.

Memories of good times
Bad times are irrelevant.
I'll always remember what we had,
Dedicated to the angel now watching from above.

Back to Me

Hugging this pillow,
Wishing it was you:
It's hard to admit, but I'm lost without you.

The loneliness kills at night.
I miss your scent.
My heart aches in the morning time.
I miss breakfast.
I miss starting off the day together.

It's no longer hard to admit I was wrong,
But it's too late now because you moved on.
A new man took my place,
And I heard he treats you better than I ever did.

I can't say I'm happy,
But I'm happy that you're happy.
I'd just be happier if you could find your way back to me.

Butterfly

You think I'm cute now,
But I remember when you used to say I was as ugly as a
caterpillar.
You say I got a sexy body,
But I remember when you use to call me the skinny kid
with the big head.
Now you're begging for some face time.

I'm not going to hold a grudge.
After all, we were just kids.
But I got to admit,
You did make my life a living hell.
But I'm past it

Let's enjoy tonight.
This is your chance to make things right.
Less teeth, more tongue:
Don't stop until all my friends come.

Accept or Decline

I need you,
But I want them.
I make love to you,
But I sex them.

You're my number one,
But I need a number two.
Got to keep things balanced:
I'm sorry, but it's just in a man's nature.

Don't take it personally.
Don't overthink it.
It's not that I'm not satisfied with you.
It's just that, once in a while, I need something different.

Get over it.
It's just life.
Accept it, or decline.

Special Treatment

I'm not one to talk about feelings.
I'm not that good at expressing that I care.
Give me a pen and paper, and I'll tell you everything you
need to hear.

When you walk by,
My heart skips a beat.
When I see you,
I can't help but stare.
I guess what I'm trying to say is, I want you,
But I don't know how to say it.

I know you got a man.
I'm not trying to come between you two.
But here's my number, in case he doesn't treat you right.
Call me, and I'll take his place in a minute and treat you
the way you ought to be treated.

Real One

Water's running low,
Lights cutting off:
We both know you can do better than that.

Settling 'cause it's becoming too difficult to find the right
guy,
Even though you know dude is no good for you.

I look at you.
I see a plant ready to blossom.
You look at me and see nothing but a friend.

I'm the one for you.
Look no further.
Tell dude it's time to leave,
Because what you two have is fake.
You got to make space for something real.

Antoni Chuck

Accidental Love

How can something so wrong feel so right?
We fell in love by accident,
But I really don't mind.

We both were in a committed relationship,
But both going nowhere.
Can't ignore destiny.
Got to pick up when fate's calling.

Like a flower, our friendship grew.
Like a tree in the spring, our love blossomed.
Something sparked, and now we're together.
Something clicked, and we can be with no other.

If you are patient enough, love will find you.
If you work hard enough, it will stay forever.
Nothing good comes without a cost.
How much do you think this relationship is valued?

A Song by the Heart

Listen to the beat as it sets the pace.
Capture the moment as the words express the thoughts.
The heart's singing.
My heart is singing,
And you're the reason why.

Filled with emotions,
Can't put into words how you make me feel.
Filled with joy; my heart's in sync with each key.

A song never heard,
A special song,
A song you inspired my heart to sing.

Best Foot Forward

Perfect,
Just perfect.
You're everything I ever wanted.

Perfect,
Just perfect.
You're everything I need.

Perfect,
Just perfect.
You're everything I ever dreamed.

Doubts,
So many doubts
That I could provide for you.

Doubts,
So many doubts
That I could be everything you need.

Fear,
So much fear.
I don't want to ruin what we have.

Chances,
Limited chances
I can't afford to miss.
I can't guarantee I will be perfect,
But I will guarantee you I'll try my best.

Beauty Comes Naturally

Why ruin your beauty with makeup?
Why degrade yourself with unnecessary piercing?
Why destroy God's art with a needle, ink, and chemicals?

You're beautiful.
Don't let anyone tell you otherwise.
You don't need artificial additions.
You're perfect in my eyes.

No makeup;
No tattoos;
No nose, lip, or tongue rings
Can make you better.

You don't need anything artificial.
Your beauty comes naturally.

One Stop Short

I noticed her brown eyes.
She couldn't keep them off me.
I noticed her red lips.
I could envision them on me.

Before I could say "Hi,"
Her stop came.
She waved bye as she slowly turned and walked out the
train door.

The Girl I Never Met

You changed my life with your smile,
Made everything okay with your presence.
You inspired feelings I thought I had lost.
You made me believe in a better today.

Rain clouds parting,
Making room for the sunlight:
Listen to the words I'm speaking.
They're coming straight from my heart.

Believe every word that I'm saying.
I need you in my life.

A Little Miracle

A miracle right before your eyes:
God's greatest gift.
Hours of pain
Quickly forgotten as you get your first look.

A future,
A project:
Someone who will always look up to you.
Someone who needs your love.
Someone who feels what you feel.

Dedicated to a true friend and her little soldier, Rashad.
Happy birthday,
And I wish you both the best.

First Cry

Waiting anxiously,
Excited and worried at the same time,
Hoping everything goes perfectly,
Hard to believe this is real at times.

A prayer,
A blessing:
There's nothing more special than the birth of a child.

It's nothing short of a miracle.
Preparing for the long journey,
Now excited to see the plant that grew from your seed.

Everyone is waiting in anticipation.
Grandma is waiting for her second grandchild.
Aunty and Uncle are waiting for another nephew they can
spoil.

Mom and Dad are growing closer together
After months of struggles and arguments.
God's gift pulls everyone closer and closer,
Reconnecting a broken family.

God's greatest gift,
A unique blessing,
A child's birth:
You'll realize it's worth it all the moment you hear the first
cry.

Grandma

To the lady of my life,
The most important person who impacted me
From birth to pre-teen.
You helped raise me the right way,
Taught me how to be self-sustaining.

You knew what was right for me,
Even when I didn't agree.
Whenever I misbehaved, you were quick to get the belt
To discipline me.

To you, I owe my honesty.
To you, I owe honor.
To you, I owe a genuine respect,
'Cause you carved a winner.

What do I give a woman who deserves the world?
What do I give her for her special day?
Nothing seems like enough,
So I pray that God blesses her with long life and happy
days.

Happy Birthday, Grandma.
Love you always.

Believe in Music

The sounds of my keyboard
Express my innermost thoughts.
A touch of the keys,
The relief the music brings
Something special when I sit and play from my feelings.

A new creation,
A new sound.
Something within this music:
Just listen to the sound.

A choir singing,
But no one is there.
Angels dancing:
Even the devil had to pause and appreciate the
atmosphere.

As I close my eyes,
These keys tell my innermost secrets.
As I touch these keys,
I present you with a gift.
As the keyboard plays,
I really start to believe in the healing power of music.

Dear Nicole

Dear Nicole,
I forgot your face, but I remember you.
I forgot your name, but I remember the time we spent.
I forgot how much I liked you, but I remember the songs
we used to sing together.

I lost everything but the memories of you,
The memories of us as kids.
I pray that one day we will be reunited,
But I fear we already have been, and I just didn't
remember you.

First Time

Can I walk you home?
Can I hold your books?
Do you mind if we hold hands
And do all the things lovers do?

Can I kiss you?
Can I touch you?
I don't really know what to do.
This is my first time.
Yes, really, my first time, and I want it to be with you.

Been talking for a while now,
I think tonight I'm going to make a move;
Reminiscing on my first time back in high school.

Crazy Chick

I know she's crazy,
But I can't help but love her obsession with me.
She'll cut a chick,
Beat a bitch, if she ever caught them looking.

You wouldn't believe the trouble she went through for me.
She's a keeper,
My right-hand chick,
But she's just a little crazy.

Always ready to brawl,
Not a day goes by without her cussing,
But she knows how to please her man.
I think I'm crazy for wanting her,
For the fact I'm not afraid to admit:
I'm in love with this crazy chick.

Love Light

I whip it out.
She gives it a taste.
I insert the plug
And light up her face.

I enjoy her moan.
I like her dirty talking.
At times, she's freakier than I am,
Inviting her girlfriends to record us.

Playground love:
Getting it on on the swing set,
Going crazy on each other as we demolish the jungle gym.

Let it rain.
Let it pour,
Leaving her leaking,
Begging no more.

Excessive sweat,
Extreme heat:
Bodies exhausted from a long night;
That's my idea of pleasure.

Antoni Chuck

Birthday Sex

Come, let me rub your shoulders.
Let me kiss your neck.
I want you all day.
I want you to enjoy this time.

It's my birthday.
It's my day.
Anything I want,
On my special day:

I want to make love all day,
Take a break,
And make love all night.

Birthday sex is the best sex,
Anything I want,
Anything I desire.

Birthday sex can't be with just anyone.
It has to be with someone special,
Someone who's worth it.

Beyond Friendship

Got to get something off my chest,
Got to tell you what's on my mind:
It's okay if you don't feel the same way,
But I got to let you know how I've been feeling inside.

At first, I thought nothing of you.
We flirted,
Said things,
But at the end of the day, I saw you as just a friend.

I was distracted by bigger boobs,
Lusting after bigger booties,
But at the end of the day, it was you I came back to.

I was easily bored by those other girls,
Talked to them for a while, then quickly forgot them.
You kept my attention all the time,
And I love you for that.

Don't want to ruin what we have,
But I don't want to keep asking "What if?"
So why don't we give it a try?
Will you be my girlfriend?

Introduction

He broke your heart
So I can mend it.

He betrayed your trust
So I can earn it.

He did all the wrong things a boyfriend can do
So you can appreciate all the right things I do.

He was immature and needed to grow up.
Forget about him;
Let me introduce you to real love.

Things I Would Do for You

For you, I'll slay the dragon.
For you, I'll battle the witch.
For you, I'll take a bite of that poisonous apple.
For you, I'll search the seas.

All I need is one kiss from you, my princess,
And I'll make your dreams come true.
All I need is for this glass slipper to fit,
And we'll be together forever.

No need for fairy godmothers,
No need for genies:
This story is bound for a happy ending
As long as you believe in it.

Antoni Chuck

Doubts

When you think I'm cheating,
When in doubt,
Just sit and think.

Who can replace you?
Who else will do the things you do,
Put up with the things you put up with?
Who can love me like you do?

When you're feeling insecure,
When you feel like I can't be trusted,
Just know you're my heartbeat.
I can't survive without you.

You're my light in this dark world.
Without you, how will I find my way?

If you ever feel like I'm falling out of love,
Just know I'm here forever
And that will never change.

If you don't hear it enough,
I love you.
If I don't express it enough,
I promise, starting from this moment, that I will change.

Words of the Wise

I want to take you away from reality,
Take you to a place where you'll feel no more pain.
I just want you to be happy.
With me, your happiness is guaranteed.

In my arms you're safe:
A kiss taking your breath away,
A touch sending chills along your body,
A feeling you never ever felt before.

Uncontrollable smiling,
Can't help but stare.
I want you so badly,
But I was told good things come to those who wait.

Simplicity

If I could get you anything in the world,
What would it be?
If I could take you anywhere you liked,
Where would it be?
If I could take you back to a moment in time,
When would it be?

Don't need any more time:
I now know what I want.
Don't need any more practice:
I've perfected my craft.

No more looking to the sky:
I found my star.
No more living in the dark:
I found my light.

Never knew till it was time:
I can't be mad forever.
Live life.
Move on.
A frown takes too much effort.

Perfection Is You and I

In case you ever second-guess us being together,
Let me give you a reason why we need each other.
In case you ever forget that I love you,
Let me remind you.
Let me make you fall in love all over again.

Believe that we will have our ups and downs,
Ins and outs,
But through it all, we have got to stay strong.
We owe it to ourselves.

I want and need you.
You need and want me.
Us together is the closest the world will get to perfection,
And perfection doesn't come easily.

I see,
I think,
I know
This is special.
What we have is unique.

Thick and Thin

Lying here,
I can't help but stare.
Can I kiss you?
Can I protect you from your worst nightmares?

When you're in need of a shoulder,
Mine is always available to you.
When you need comforting,
I'll always be right next to you.
When you're struggling and feel like you can't make it,
I'll be there to pick you up.
I'll be your biggest motivator.
I won't let you give up.

I want to be the one you can always count on,
the one who's always there for you,
Your better half,
The one who completes you.

3:04 a.m.

Waking up this morning
With you on my mind:
Last night, I barely had any sleep.
You kept my thoughts occupied.

I know we just met,
But I feel like I know you.
I can see the loneliness in your face.
Can I please rescue you?

Been doing things out of the ordinary:
I'm trying to impress you.
I would give you anything you like,
But first off, I'm going to make you fall in love with me.

Sooner Than Later

I know it's been many years since we last spoke,
But I still want you.
Seeing you the other day
Brought back so many memories.

We argued, went our separate ways,
But you know we were bound to cross paths again.
You want to take it slow, get to know each other as friends
again before we go any farther.

I would say it's a good idea, but I would be lying.
Your body is tempting me more and more by the day.
I want to love you.
Can I please love you?
I'd rather we get together sooner than later.

Gone

Heartbroken over a text,
Pouring my heart out online:
She won't reply to me.
She keeps ignoring my calls.

No explanation,
All she said was "We're done."
I figured out why:
Her friends asking what took her so long.

I go on, pretending I don't care,
But deep down, it's killing me.
I know I did her wrong,
But she didn't have to leave me,
At least not like this.

She crossed the bridge and burnt it before I noticed.
She left me on the other side and kept running.
I'm usually playing the role of the asshole, but I guess the
tables turned.
Now I'm here experiencing what she experienced,
Watching helplessly as my heart burns.

She's gone.
Nothing was said.
She's gone,
And she took the best part of me.

Antoni Chuck

She's gone,
No explanation,
But I know what I did.
I guess the time it took her to leave really caught me
off-guard.

Heartbroken,
Lonely:
She left me in the dark.
Understandable,
But she didn't have to leave me,
At least not the way she did.

Texting,
Calling,
Emailing her, but no reply.

She's serious.
She's really gone.
The best part of me is really gone.

Happily Ever After

Met you in my dream last night,
But you walked away before I could get your name.
It's funny how I found you in this club tonight.
It's like destiny called my name.

Can I get you a drink?
What would you like?
I really want to get to know you.
What are you doing later on tonight?

Save your number as the girl of my dreams:
I would do whatever it takes to put a smile on your face.
I'll take you anywhere you like.
Just say the word and we'll be on our way.

It's like my dream continued into reality.
Never believed in fairytales,
But then the craziest thing happened;
We passed a billboard saying "The prince and princess
lived happily ever after."

PART TWO

Poverty & Greed

Money Never Sleeps

Money never sleeps.
You'll go crazy trying to catch up to it.
Is it worth all the risks?
Is it worth everything important?

Money never sleeps.
You'll go crazy trying to keep it.
Money is an unfaithful partner,
Inconsiderate of its lovers' feelings.

Money never sleeps.
Greed is an incurable and highly infectious global
epidemic.
No matter how much you have,
You'll never have enough of it.

Society

Exhausted,
Body don't want to go no more,
Knees hurting,
I'm here breaking my back, just to be considered poor.

So many hours gone
And nothing to show for it.
Bill collectors keep calling,
And my bank account is running on empty.

As soon as a check comes in, it's gone.
Living life from hand to mouth,
Sometimes hand doesn't have anything for mouth.
Sometimes I question how I'm surviving.
I can't begin to tell how hard it is living in this society.

Land of B. S. and Z.

In the land of the blood suckers and zombies,
No one is around to save you.
You're at their mercy.

A lifeless body roaming,
You can't expect them to have morals.
They only need one thing to survive,
And it's something you and I have.

In the land of the blood suckers and zombies,
No one and nothing is safe.
Everything you work hard for, they're going to take.

No options,
Just demands:
You'll die if you fail to comply.

It's just another night,
And you're just another victim
In the land of the blood suckers and zombies.

Questions of Hate

Will they hate me when I get out?
Will they despise me when I'm on top?
Will they be jealous, and hope I fall?
Or will they be happy that at least one of us got out?

You can dodge some of the hate,
But you can't avoid human nature.
Not everyone likes to see someone they know succeed,
So you can expect those people to go around starting
rumors.

Lift your head.
Keep it high.
Don't let them get to you.
No matter what they throw at you,
You will survive.

Dream big.
When they tell you that you can't,
Set your goals even higher.
Tell them *can't* is not a word
And *failure* isn't in your vocabulary.

Three White Palaces

You're not from where I'm from,
So how can you relate?
Never had a hard day in your life,
So how can you talk about struggling?

Couldn't survive a day in my shoes.
Couldn't survive a night in the place I'm from.
Talk is talk.
Words don't change anything around here.
Action is needed just to survive here.

Never gone, but I'm always leaving.
Never got, but I'm always sharing.
You see, they need that selflessness,
Someone to show they're still human.

Goodbye, Misery

Money talks,
And right now, it appears to be shouting over me.
I'm talking, but you can't hear.
I'm telling you how I feel,
And you just ignore me.

Feeling like I've been pushed aside,
No longer important,
No longer somebody.

Feeling like a stranger in my own home.
Strangers treat me better than my own blood.
Feeling far from a family.

Happy
Is something we just aren't.
Grudges and jealousy are all I see.
I can't live like this.
That's why I'm leaving.
Goodbye, misery.

The Value of Memories

When you take your last breath,
All material things will become worthless.
All the earthly things will be forgotten.
You'll find the real treasure is memories.

In your last moment, memories are all you have.

PART THREE

Revolution

The Illusion of Freedom

The question is, "Why?"
The answer is, "Why not?"
Far from free,
But not locked up.

The mind roams freely,
But the body is trapped in this dreadful place.
Free to speak,
But be careful what you say.
You wouldn't want to piss off the wrong people, now.
They just might use their freedom of speech to verbally
consent your death.

Free
As the caged bird,
Free to sing any song,
Free as long as you're singing your master's chosen songs.

Antoni Chuck

Rebel

Sharing a spliff with Bob Marley,
Listening to Martin Luther King Jr. preach,
Loading guns with Malcolm X
While plotting strategies with Che:

A rebel in a new time.
It's time we restore our order.
We're lacking a spark.
We can't keep following orders.

Rebel,
Think for yourself.
Rebel,
Don't let them brainwash you.
Rebel,
We won't survive if we don't come together as one to
destroy the new world order.

Marked Man

A marked man,
Someone's target,
I can't sleep,
Worrying if this day might be my last.

Dreaming of a symbol,
Waking up
To notice half of it is on my hands.

What does this mean?
Am I truly a marked man?

Soldier in Time

A soldier in time:
A man,
A kid.

Coming from a place where hell was my home,
And the devil was taking care of me.

A sacrifice,
A bond.
Never knowing of heaven,
Never understanding peace.

Always fighting,
Arguing,
Never experiencing happiness.

A soldier in time,
Bred,
Carved into a monster.

A soldier in time,
The day is quickly approaching,
The day that the leash won't be strong enough to restrain
this monster.

Price Check

Eyes are always watching.
Can't you hear them whispering,
Always scrutinizing me?

I'm human.
I'm a man.
I make mistakes.
I'm far from perfect,
Yet they still place me on the highest pedestal.

Every move I make,
There's someone talking about it.
Every time I leave, there's always someone following.

Is this the price to pay?
Can I get a price check on freedom?

Perfect Day

A perfect day:
What an illusion.
The sun is shining, yet its freezing.

Fun in the snow;
It's overrated.
Walking around is now an ancient activity.
Waiting in front of doors, expecting them to automatically
open,
Taking a while to realize you still have to use your hands
on some doors.

Is this what we've come to?
Is this what we consider to be advanced?
Can't live life in the wild,
But in space we can certainly survive.

Schools teaching useless lessons,
Keeping real knowledge from a simple man.
How is it that a man considered a failure in the academic
world
Became an international legend?

Rebellion

No more will it hurt again.
No more will the sun shine.
If you know what's good for you,
You'll run for the light.

Can't see a thing
Blinded by this fog.
Somewhere at this very moment,
Someone is calling for a savior.

A cover-up,
A conspiracy,
They're trying to sneak something into this world
undetected.

Can't feel my face.
Can't open my eyes.
My body feels like a heavy weight
That I can no longer lift up.

They caught me,
But not before I spread the word to you.
Wake up.
Gather the rest.
It's about time for a rebellion.

Antoni Chuck

New World

Reinvention of a new generation,
Tired of the same old cards being reshuffled.

It's time for a new deck,
Rebirth of the radicals.
It's been too long since the last Million Man March.

It's time for change.
The old system will be at the mercy of the young.

A new era:
Revolutionary is the perfect word.
We can never go back now.
This war will bring forth a new world.

PART FOUR

Reality Check

Reality Check

My stomach hurting,
My head's spinning.
My hands shaking.
Thinking of what could be.
What could happen?

Never thought,
Now I'm left with regrets.
Can't be mad at anyone but myself.

Premature trust,
False sense of security,
Now I'm left to face the permanent consequences.

Many days I hope,
Many days I pray,
I wish it was all a dream,
But everyday reality sets in.

Antoni Chuck

Hero or Villain

Vision of me taking a bullet,
Falling down bleeding,
Saying to myself *I can't die now*.
Hearing his voice, I was well motivated.
As soon as he turned his back,
I grabbed the gun; put one in his chest and two in his
head,
Then I collapsed again.

Am I a hero?
Or an accidental villain?
I saved many lives,
But I took one.
Am I right, even though I'm wrong?

Considered a hero,
Even though I'm not much different than a villain.

Crazy World

Sheet covering the body,
The paramedic's hands covered with blood,
The friends and family of the victim crying in disbelief
As the anchorman announces another untimely death:

It appears to be a recurrence.
Yellow tape and chalk is becoming way too normal.
A life is not worth much these days.
We know the price of all material things
But have forgotten the value of each other.

A fatherless son,
A motherless daughter:
No parents should outlive their kids.
Never should they be carrying their child to the graveyard.

It's a crazy world we live in,
And lately it's harder and harder to survive.
It's a crazy world we live in,
And at the rate we're going,
Who will survive?

Antoni Chuck

Moment of Acceptance

A moment of peace,
A moment of love,
Just a moment of happiness:
That's all I need

Been distracted,
Lost my way,
Forgot the important things,
Gone astray.

Caught up in this world,
Doing everything wrong,
Leaving my footprints in the sand
As I walk toward the ocean.

Heartbreak Hotel

Check in on time.
Get comfortable.
Give your heart to me.
Don't worry, I won't break it.

Let me help you with your excess baggage.
Let me show you to your room.
I don't require a tip.
All I need is your complete attention.

Watch as the sun sets on the balcony.
In the distance you can see the monsters marching in.
Only human among vampires;
How do you think it's going to end?

You're just another victim of the Heartbreak Hotel

Antoni Chuck

At War with My Enemies

Last night, I dreamt I was arguing
Face to face with my enemies,
Got tired and walked away.
Little did I know, things were far from over.

I was brought to the back of my old school,
Where I was with my girl and only child.
Things fast-forwarded a bit,
And I saw my enemies passing by.
Thinking nothing of it, I left to go deal with something.

Next thing I know, I'm running,
Running for my life.
Met up with my old principal,
Had a conversation.

Before I knew it, I received word that they got my girl and
killed my child.
Now things are becoming clear.
I now know what I must do.

Face to face with my worst nightmare.
He had a knife, and he shouted, "I'm going to kill you."
He stabbed me once,
But I didn't feel anything.
He tried again, and before he knew it, I took his life.

Reality Check

I could hear the sirens getting closer and closer,
So I emptied my pockets.
Raised my hands, and surrendered.

Heading to jail,
Placed in the same cell as the man I just killed,
I got my corner.
He got his.
Not a word was said,
Just a cruel, cold stare.

Out of nowhere came the knife I used to kill him.
I took it, approached him.
And finished what he started.

Covered with blood,
The cell door slid open.
As I walked out, I looked back at the body
And realized it was me I had just murdered.

Careful Planning

Going to sleep thinking everything was fine.
Next thing I knew, I started dreaming,
Started piecing things together.

It's too late now,
As I try to get up,
Feeling lightheaded,
Watching as they hide their smirks.

Can't believe I didn't see this,
Should've known this was coming.
Them being peaceful was all an act,
And this was the result of careful planning.

I try to fight it.
I've got to survive this.
I'm not ready for death,
So I lay back down, pray to God,
And now I'm writing this.

Perfect Crime

Blinded by lust,
I was ignoring all the signs.
I found myself a pathological liar.
The scary thing is, I still don't know her motive.

Blinded by happiness,
It felt good to fill that lonely void.
I had my doubts about her,
But I had no proof to confront her with.

Now she just up and left,
After cleaning my pipe.
Texted me hours later, saying what we did wasn't right.

I'm scared right now,
A little confused.
I really hope she didn't do the unthinkable.
I really hope she didn't just commit the perfect crime.

Obsession

Obsession with numbers,
Obsession with dates,
Obsession with memories,
Hoping everything stays the same.

Remembering faces,
Forgetting names.
Memory is a funny skill:
If you master it, no one can ever forget your name.

Living forever,
Outliving time.
Why are we so obsessed with living?
Is it because we don't know what comes after life?

Can we live on another planet?
Are there other life forms out in space?
How about if we take care of the planet we have now,
And focus on unlocking all her secrets and mysteries?

Tossing and Turning

Tossing and turning,
Not knowing what's on my mind.
Can't think,
Can't sleep,
I appear lost in time.

I know what I want to do,
But for some strange reason, I can't do it.
I walk around, back and forth,
Pacing by myself,
Looking to the sky for answers,
Wasting time,
Valuable time.
There is no explanation for what I've been doing.

The Cure

To be told you can't,
To be told you're a failure,
To be told you'll never amount to anything,
To be around all this hatred:

Motivation,
A reason to succeed.
Nothing will hurt them more than seeing you achieve your
dreams.

Never fall for their traps.
Never give in to their demands.
Keep doing what makes you happy.
Success is the best medicine for this epidemic we call
hatred.

Sunrise

Mentally exhausted,
Physically sick,
Don't know how much more I can take.
I can't keep doing this.

Wasting my life away,
Throwing away precious time,
I can't keep doing things this way.
It's about time certain things in my life changed.

Stressing,
Worrying about things,
Getting angry
'Cause it didn't turn out the way I planned.

Envisioning success,
By example I will lead:
No more excuses,
No more outbreaks of childish behavior.

Stand up,
Face what's ahead,
Never let someone else's mistakes prevent you from getting
where you want to get.
Never give up.
Never let the rain destroy a perfect day.
Always make the best of what you have,
And remember the sun always returns each day.

Leave Me Alone

A bitter taste:
I don't feel like fighting anymore.
The pain is unbearable.
Who can I trust?
The world is so cold.

They ask.
I give.
They take advantage.
My inner self points and laughs, saying, "I told you so."

Don't want to go any farther.
I feel like giving up.
Life's becoming overwhelming,
All these years and no progress.

Been away so long
That I'm becoming separated.
I've lost basic interest.
I speak to no one.

Prefer a dark room,
No lights,
No company,
Just peace and quiet.

Leave me alone with my music.
Leave me alone to die.
Don't need no help.
Don't need no one.
People are only good for hurt and disappointment,
And I want neither.

The Prayer

Lord, forgive them,
For they know not what they are doing.
They don't know plotting against me will lead to their
destruction.

Lord, help me forgive them,
For I'm deeply hurt
And contemplating revenge.

Lord, I need your help,
Your guidance,
For before me are two paths,
And neither has a sign.

One has a dirt road,
And the other is paved.
One has extreme heat,
And the other, extreme cold.

Looking at both options,
I know there are many things,
Many obstacles ahead.

What I'm asking,
What I need from you, Lord,
Is for you to guide me in the right direction.
Help me fulfill my destiny.
Help me become the real me.

On My Two Feet

On the edge,
Being pressured to jump.
Looking down,
And nothing but negative thoughts fill my mind.

Wonder what they would say now if they could see me?
Would they think differently?
Or would life be the same?

Is this what my life came to?
Is this what I really want to do?
Looking for answers to fall from the sky,
Thinking,
Feeling empty,
Can't bear to close my eyes.

Looked straight ahead,
I faced my worst fears,
Took that first step, and landed right on my two feet.